Edward L Anderson

Six Weeks in Norway

Edward L Anderson

Six Weeks in Norway

ISBN/EAN: 9783743337053

Manufactured in Europe, USA, Canada, Australia, Japa

Cover: Foto ©Andreas Hilbeck / pixelio.de

Manufactured and distributed by brebook publishing software
(www.brebook.com)

Edward L Anderson

Six Weeks in Norway

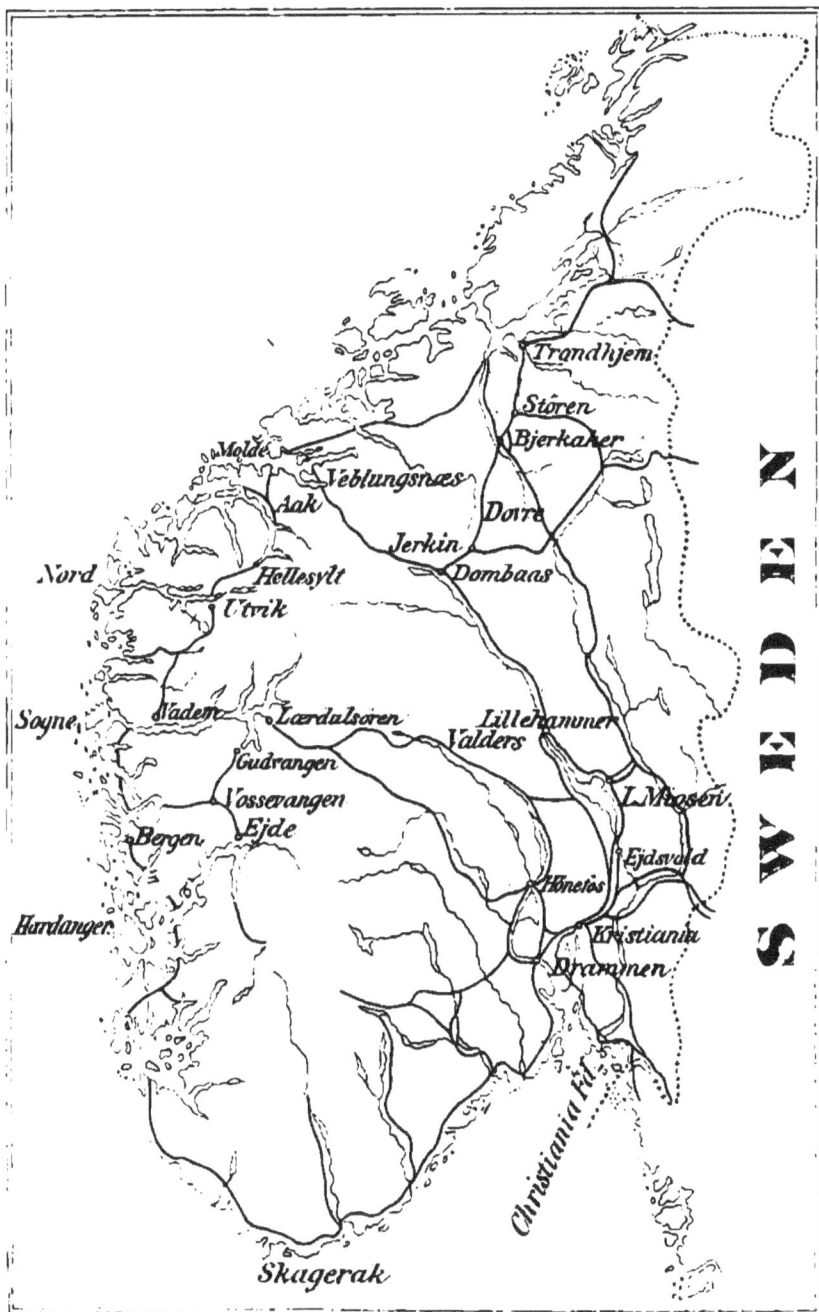

Trondhjem

Stören

Bjerkaker

Molde

Veblungsnæs

Aak

Dovre

Jerkin

Nord

Hellesylt

Dombaas

Utvik

Soyne

Naden

Lærdalsören

Lillehammer

Valders

Gudvangen

Vossevangen

L. Miösen

Ejde

Bergen

Ejdsvold

Hönefos

Hardanger

Kristiania

Drammen

Christiania Fd.

Skagerak

S W E D E N

The Krebs Lithographing Company, Cincinnati.

SIX WEEKS

IN

NORWAY

ERSON,

Ballads."

CLARKE & CO.

1877.

TO

CONSUL GERHARD GADE,

OF

CHRISTIANIA.

CONTENTS.

SIX WEEKS IN NORWAY.

CHAPTER I.

FROM COPENHAGEN TO CHRISTIANIA.

O F the various routes by which the traveler
may reach Norway, that which lies through
Copenhagen is to be preferred, for the voyage to
Christiania, from whence a tour of the country
should begin, is of only twenty hours' duration,
while the line of steamers from Hull, large and
stanch vessels, spend three or four days in those
rough northern seas. I confess that my expe-
rience of the route here recommended was not
a pleasant one, but, since I passed over it, the
large and swift ship "Christiania" has been

put upon the line, and the miseries of the Skagerack have been alleviated.

At noon of the 9th day of July, 1875, my wife
and I found ourselves upon the little steamship
"Aarhuus," gliding out of the harbor of Copenhagen. For some hours we coasted close to the
eastern shore, of Seeland, which presented a
thickly-settled but rather uninteresting country.
About four o'clock we passed Elsinore, with its
picturesque castle, fondly believed in by all tourists to be the scene of Shakespeare's Hamlet.
From this point the strait widens, and is known
as the Cattegat. Here, in the winter months, is
felt the force of the storms sweeping from the
north, making these waters exceedingly dangerous to the small vessels that venture upon them.
Indeed, although it was midsummer, we did not
find the sea very quiet. My wife sought refuge
in the small cabin set apart for the ladies, while
I, unable to remain in the close and crowded sa-
loon, lay down upon the hard deck. The clouds,
that had long been threatening, poured down
upon us in a cold rain, and the "Aarhuus" began

the most singular acrobatic performances, doing everything but complete somersaults. The vessel was crowded with passengers, most of whom had followed my example in coming upon deck to be ill.

We experienced a slight relief about midnight, when we stopped at Gothenburg; but when we were well out in the Skagerack, the motions of the vessel and our discomforts were increased. Daylight brought no change, except the satisfaction of beholding the sufferings of each other. The day wore away, and about four o'clock the gentleman who was ill at the bow, called out the joyful news that land was in view.

Before us were the green hills of Norway, growing into bare peaks in the distance. Against a rocky barrier, that defended the coast, the mad sea raged and rushed, breaking into columns of spray, and falling back in sheets of foam. At the extremity of a shallow bay, the little town of Laurvig, with its red-tiled roofs, lay smiling at the threatening ocean.

We remained at Laurvig long enough for a

sea-conquered viking to drag himself on to the pier, and then once more into the Skagerack. But only for a short time; for, passing a point of land, and steaming between two dangerous looking rocks, we entered Christiania fiord, and were once more in smooth water.

It was now six o'clock, but it was still broad, glaring daylight; for the storm had ceased, and the clouds had been dissipated by the warm sun. Christiania fiord has none of the characteristics that have made the western bays of Norway celebrated for their grandeur of scenery, but presents, notwithstanding, many beautiful views, reminding the American of the upper Hudson. Many bold islands, some of them inhabited, appear as we advance, and these give a charm that is wanting to our river.

It was midnight when we reached Christiania, but there was still light enough to see the vessels in the harbor, and to admire the old fortress of Akershuus, that pretends to guard the town. Civil customs-officers hurriedly examined our luggage, and a short walk through the deserted streets brought us to the Victoria Hotel, one of the best inns in Northern Europe.

Christiania is a well-built city, beautifully situated about the head of the fiord, seventy miles from the sea, and, it is asserted, has a population of 80,000 souls. It is the first commercial port of 'Norway, and supplies nearly the whole of the southern part of the country with foreign imports. The harbor is without a rival, and the flags of all nations may be seen upon the shipping. Many of the public edifices are of imposing appearance, and the residences in the suburbs exhibit taste and wealth. The hills in the vicinity furnish many pleasing prospects, and the roads are excellent. Three miles from the city rises Frognersœter, from whence an extended and varied view may be had. The city, the silver fiord dotted with islands, the pine-clad hills, and the distant peaks, with their snowy caps, are presented to the eye. Overlooking the fiord, and in a setting of emerald trees, is Oscar's Hall, a summer palace of the king. Here may be seen some of the master-pieces of Norwegian paint-

ers, landscapes by Gude, and pictures of peasant
life by Tidemand.

During the morning of our arrival, I called
upon Mr. Gerhard Gade, consul for the United
States, and found him ready to give us every assistance in preparing for our journey. I can not
express our obligations to this gentleman for his
attentions and kindness, and it was at his delightful country-house, "Frogner," that we first
learned that northern hospitality does not partake
of the coldness of the climate.

I learned from Mr. Gade that the roads had
been so greatly improved of late years, that
upon all the main routes, and indeed wherever
wheeled vehicles could be used at all, a light
carriage might be substituted for the inconven-
ient and wearying two-wheeled carriole men-
tioned in the guide-book. This was a very
agreeable piece of information, for I had looked
with dread upon the long rides, day after day,
in a seat that gives no support to the back.
I found that the carriole is still used by the English, who do not believe in innovations, and who

pride themselves upon following the customs of a country, even at the expense of comfort; but for the natives who can afford to travel in a more luxurious manner, it is a thing of the past. So far from the carriole being a necessity, it is even proposed that a diligence shall be run next year between Christiania and Throndhjem, crossing the Dovre-field over one of the heaviest roads in the country.

There are few railroad lines at present in operation in Norway, but the system of posting has been brought almost to perfection. At points seven miles apart, or as near that distance from each other as is practicable, posting-houses have been established, where the traveler may obtain fresh horses and lodging, if he require it, at prices· fixed by the local government. These stations are, for the most part, the homes of the farmers, and the accommodations, as might be expected, are of a primitive character, but they are the best that the country can afford, and the guest is always sure of civility and attention. The Norwegian peasant—and except on the coast

there are few towns—is proud of his ancestry
and of his hard-won freedom, but, unless his dig-
nity is touched, he is the most polite and hospita-
ble of mortals.

It is necessary for the tourist in Norway to
have a courier who understands the language,
and, as competent guides can be found in Christiania, I advise the traveler to procure one after
he arrives in the country.   I believe that all
Norwegians are thoroughly honest, even to the
couriers, and I heartily recommend Matthias
Johanssen, of Christiania,· as a most capable,
energetic, and trustworthy man.   Indeed, I can
hardly imagine a stranger seeing Norway to the
greatest advantage without having the ready
and well-informed Johanssen at his side, and
under his care there are no discomforts.

We spent a week pleasantly in Christiania, and
the evening before we were to take our departure
for the country, Johanssen called us down into the
court yard of the hotel to examine the prepara-
tions for our journey, for which he alone was re-
sponsible.   We found a light calèche carriage,

closely packed with preserved meats, crackers, etc., while an ingenious contrivance, pendant from the dash-board, held a dozen sma'l bottles of Bordeaux wine. My fears in regard to the safety of these latter fragile goods were set at rest when Johanssen assured me that Norwegian horses would not kick. A board fastened to the rear axle was intended for the single trunk that we were to carry.

After the inspection, the carriage, thus richly laden, was taken and placed upon an open platform car, where it remained undisturbed throughout the night. Not an article was missing in the morning. And I may as well state here that it was our custom to leave our property in the carriage, as it stood by the roadside, night after night, at the inn door, and our faith in the honesty of the people was never shaken.

We had determined that the first division of our journey should be through Gudbrandsdalen, over the Dovre-field to Throndhjem, and we were to take advantage of the railroad as far as Eidsvold, at the foot of Miosen lake, a distance of about thirty miles. As we were to make an early start, we bade our *adieux*, and went to rest long before the summer day was over.

CHAPTER II.

FROM CHRISTIANIA OVER THE DOVRE-FIELD TO THRONDHJEM.

AT seven o'clock on the morning of July 18th, we took the train for Eidsvold, at the terminus of the road, and accomplished the journey in three hours. Near at hand, the pretty little steamer "King Oscar" lay in the Vormen river, ready to take us to Lillehamar, at the head of Lake Miosen.

Johanssen had our carriage placed on the fore-deck, while we, under the "grateful shade" of an awning, rested on the quarter-deck, happy in our anticipations of a novel tour. With a bearing that would have been becoming in the cap-

tain of a first-class man-of-war, the master of the
"Oscar" gave orders to cast off, and we rapidly
slipped out of the river into the lake. Miosen is
a beautiful sheet of water, seventy miles in
length, the greatest breadth being but ten miles.
The hills on the lower part are precipitous, and
Skreibjerget, on the western shore, is a mountain
of the respectable height of 2,200 feet. As we
proceed north, the hillsides are less steep, and
are dotted with fields of grain and pasture. At
the widest part of the lake, about midway, is the
island of Helgo, a splendid farm, and formerly
the estate of one of the wealthy nobles.

Four arches of the ancient cathedral, built in the
year 1152 by the bishop, who was afterward Pope
Hadrian IV, have a commanding position on a
point of land running into the lake from the site
of ancient Hamar, and show that a splendid edifice once occupied the site. After passing the
island of Helgo, the lake narrows to a uniform
width of about two miles, until it meets the river
Laagen at Lillehamar. While we were on the
latter part of the journey, the master of the vessel

approached me, and in very good English asked me if I knew General So and So, or Colonel Blank, or Major Ditto, and seemed very much disappointed that I did not have the honor of an acquaintance with any of these heroes, who, he assured me, were fellow-countrymen of mine. It turned out that the skipper's hobby was the collection of visiting cards; and as every American who travels abroad takes a title, if he may by chance lay any claim to one, he had a very pretty collection of the names of the American nobility. I think that he threw my card, which had simply the prefix of "Mr.," into the lake.

Lillehamar, which we reached about seven o'clock in the evening, is one of the few inland towns of Norway, and boasts only of 1,700 inhabitants. It is built on the hillside, and will not cause much loss should it fall into the lake, as is reasonably to be expected. I do not know how bad was the rival house that we saw a cockney driving to as we entered the "Victoria," but I feel sure that he had a better supper and a softer

bed than we found. I did not try the breakfast,
for which we were roused, as I preferred taking
the chances for such food as the farmers could
offer, or that the courier might prepare on the
road.

We made an early start, for at six o'clock we
were seated in the carriage. Johanssen mounted
the box beside the post-boy, and with a whip-
cracking that would have satisfied an Italian *vet-
turino*, we began our journey on wheels. Our
road lay up through Gudbrandsdalen, one of
the grand valleys that make Norway habitable,
which, with its continuation, the Romsdal, ex-
tends from the upper end of Lake Miosen to the
sea at Veblungsnœs, and is the great artery of
trade. The Laagen river, that takes its rise in
the Lesjeverksvand, flows down the length of this
valley, while the Rauma, that flows from the
same source, runs northwardly down the Romsdal. These rivers, swift and strong, add much
to the beauty of the valley, and they keep the
traveler company through the journey from lake
to sea.

We bowled along right merrily in the bright clear sunshine, the road being as smooth as a floor. Nine miles, which we made in less than an hour, brought us to Fossegarden, but as the station was some little distance from the road, my wife and I remained in the carriage, while the courier went after fresh horses. These quickly appeared. We paid the post-boy, who had come with us from Lillehamar, a sum amounting to about one dollar for each seven miles, and the inevitable drink-money, and, with a very sleepy looking youth to look after our new team, we resumed our journey. The Laagen, near this point, becomes very rapid, and the whirling waters are said to be alive with trout. The hills on either hand increase in size and grandeur as we proceed, the valley decreasing in width. We drove the ten miles to Holmen in a little more than an hour, and for the first time had the opportunity of examining a "station." The building was of squared logs, as are all of the stations in Norway, though some are weather-boarded, and contained four rooms.

In one of these the family lived ; the remaining rooms were at the service of the traveling public. Numerous out-buildings flanked the house, and the large hay-barns indicated the length of the winter. The furniture was of the simplest description, and there were no unnecessary articles. This may be taken as an example of the poorer road-stations, for some of those that have become popular are very fair inns, both in regard to size and comforts. Holmen is too near Lillehamar to attract any great amount of custom. At this place I, for the first time, tasted Norwegian beer —an excellent drink, that may be had of good quality all over the country. Passing through three other stations, the scenery increasing in wildness and interest as we advanced, we reached Oien about six o'clock in the evening, having traveled fifty miles without experiencing the slightest fatigue.

Oien is one of the best stations on this route. We were shown into a neat room, simply furnished, but arranged with a taste that would do credit to a Norman farm-wife. The beds were

clean and inviting, while carefully arranged cur-
tains screened the windows.

Dinner was announced very shortly after our
arrival, and we were served by a trim girl,
who might have been a graduate from a French
restaurant. The meal was the result of a com-
bination of our tins with what we had found
in the house, and was worthy of the appetites
that were ready for it. Fish of the finest quality may be obtained all over Norway. The
smaller streams furnish trout in abundance, the
lakes and rivers are full of salmon-trout, while
the royal salmon is ready to leap to the fly from
every stream that flows into the sea.

Six o'clock found us again upon the road ; for,
as this is the season for travel, it is well to be out
early, so that horses may be procured without
delay. A short distance from the first station,
Storklevstad, we came to a monument erected by
the side of the road to the memory of Colonel
Sinclair, a Scotchman, who, in 1612, with nine
hundred followers, attempted to cross Norway to
the aid of the Swedish king, and being opposed

in the Kringlen pass by about three hundred peasants, was slain, with all his men, by rocks and timber that were thrown down the mountain side upon the road they could not leave. Fourteen miles further on, we came to the Kringlen pass, the alleged scene of this disaster.

The mountains had been increasing in size and improving in form since morning, and the valley had become little more than a defile for the roaring Laagen. After passing Laurgaard, the scenery becomes very wild, the precipices rising up like walls on either hand, the road crossing the stream from side to side to find a place for itself. This part of the valley, known as the Rusten pass, is a grand gorge, and every feature stands out in my memory as I recall it.

Six o'clock found us at Tofte-moen, about forty-five miles from our starting place of the morning. The accommodations at this station were not so good as those at Oien, but then the honor of being entertained by a lineal descendant of King Harfaagr, as was claimed for himself by the station-master, was some compensation.

The bedsteads offered by this royal host were rudely made, and the mattresses were bags of straw, but his majesty was polite and the princess attentive, and as we were very sleepy, we passed a reasonably comfortable night.

Before morning several travelers arrived, so that, to secure horses, we were compelled to make another early start. The ponies used in Gudbrandsdalen are not, as a rule, of the true Norwegian breed, but have greater size, from an infusion of the Danish horse, to the injury, in my opinion, of the original stock. The true Norwegian horse is now found only on the western fiords. He seldom rises fourteen hands in height; must be of some shade of dun, with a black stripe leading from his forehead down his back to the end of his tail. The legs are either black or barred with black. This animal has great endurance, a perfect temper, and will fatten on food that would scarcely nourish a rabbit. I brought a pair from the Sondmore district home with me, and I congratulate myself upon the possession of them. There is a horse found in Gudbrandsdalen, peculiar to that district, that has great size, with symmetry, but he is very different from the Danish animal, which resembles a saw-horse, and has but little more life.

Crack! goes the whip, and off we whirl, at the rate of ten miles an hour, down to Dombass, at the foot of the Dovre-field. Here we leave Gudbrandsdalen for the present, and, with the smallest horses we have yet used, essay the mountain road.

The long, steep hill proved too much for our ponies, and Mrs. Anderson and I left the empty carriage to come on by slow stages, while we attacked the Dovre-field on foot. Beautiful wild-flowers, of the most delicate shapes and of the richest coloring, literally bordered the road, and I culled at least twenty varieties. The trees decreased in size as we advanced, and, after walking four or five miles, we reached the plateau, a treeless, dreary moorland of very uneven surface. The Dovre-field, at the place where the road crosses it, is about thirty-five miles from base to base; the table-land, or *field* proper, being about eighteen miles in breadth.

It was not a long time before Johanssen came up with the carriage, and, after giving the ponies a short rest, we were soon rolling along the road, that, taking advantage of the character of the ground, was nearly level, although there is a gradual ascent until Jerkin is reached. Seven miles from Dombass, and more than one thousand feet above it, is the station of Fokstuen, one of the dreariest places imaginable; the former station being the nearest dwelling-house, while Jerkin is fourteen miles further on across the *field*. In the summer time, when these upland pastures or *sæters* furnish grass, the people of Fokstuen have for neighbors the peasant women who care for the cattle. These cowherds live in miserable little hovels, roughly made of planking placed upright. But this sæter-life is only for two months. For the remainder of the year the station-master and his family are the only inhabitants of this bleak region.

By the time we had reached Jerkin, which is

more than three thousand feet higher than Dombass, it was so cold that we determined to leave the road, and make ourselves as comfortable as the place would permit. There are two living-houses here, besides the numerous out-buildings common to the farms. Jerkin is one of the oldest stations in Norway, is placed at the crossing of two important roads, and has a much better reputation for comforts than it deserves. Indeed, it is so popular that we found that ten or twelve travelers had already settled upon this station for the night, and the capacities of the inn were tried.

We ran away from the lazy ones very early in the morning, and securing the best horses, continued our journey. As we passed around a hill, about two miles from the station, Snehatta (Snow Cap) burst upon our admiring eyes. This mountain, although it is barely 8,000 feet above the sea level, is magnificent, by reason of its form and the boldness with which it stands up out of the *field.* It is a truncated pyramid in shape, with three bastard peaks. Near the road, the

Kolla, like a sugar-loaf in shape, rises up to the height of six thousand feet, while the Knudsho, on the right-hand side of the road, is only ninety feet less. This is by far the finest part of the Dovre-field, for the foreground is filled with magnificent, moss-covered bowlders that are worthy of the grand peaks that surround them on all sides. Now we begin the descent, and the little brook that sings by the roadside will very soon grow into the rapid Driva, that has carved a way for us down the steep mountain side. We were soon shut in by the valley, and the mountains seemed to grow as we looked on them. After leaving Kongsvold, the valley increased in beauty. At one point near Drivstuen, the river rushed noisily through the deep gorge that confined it, and it was necessary to cut a bed for the road out of the mountain side. Then the valley opened out, until at Aune, where we stopped to take lunch, there were good broad fields.

I tried the Norwegian cheeses, of which there are two kinds, at this station. The one looks and tastes as if it were made of a mixture of brown

sugar and rancid lard. The other, less objec-
tionable, was of a spongy consistency, and had
no taste at all.

At this point we left the valley of the Driva,
and passing by Stuen, struck the valley of the
Orkla river near Austbjerg. The latter part of
this stage passes through some very fine scenery.
From Austbjerg the road continues on the same
level, while the river falling rapidly forms a deep
and wide valley just beneath ; the splendid snow-
clad mountains on the opposite side showing to
great advantage. At one point on this stage the
roadway is cut into the mountain side, and the
river flows eight hundred feet below.

At six o'clock, in a drenching rain, we reached
Bjerkaker, and were very glad to find a good
fire in the kitchen, by which we could warm and
dry ourselves. The dinner was soon served, and
as we had come more than fifty miles, it was not
long before we retired. Not to sleep, alas! for
our bed-room was separated from the dining-hall
by a thin board partition, and two young English-
men, who had been fishing in the Orkla, and

had come to the station for dinner, kept up their sporting reminiscences in loud tones until a late hour.

I wish to warn the reader against thinking that these stations in any way resemble towns. A station is simply a farm-house that is offered to the traveling public, and although its long name may appear grandly on the maps of Norway, there is not one, except Lillehamar, that rises to the rank of a village.

We had to make but two more stages before we should reach Storen, the terminus of the railway, about thirty miles from Throndhjem. At Presthus, the last station on the route, we met a young bridal couple, traveling by carrioles, who had just finished their first stage. The lady, who appeared to be already fatigued, carried a worthless cur in her arms, about as troublesome an ornament as could be well imagined. I pictured to myself that dog flying through space over the precipice near Austbjerg, if it survived so far.

We had an early dinner at Storen, and at seven o'clock took the train for Throndhjem.

The railway, a fine piece of engineering, follows the valley of a river that affords many beautiful views. At ten o'clock we reached the venerable city, and found comfortable rooms and a good table at the hotel Angleterre.

CHAPTER III.

FROM THRONDHJEM OVER THE DOVRE-FIELD TO AAK IN ROMSDAL.

I SPOKE of Throndhjem as venerable; but, except the cathedral, which is only about eight hundred years old, there are few houses of any great age, as the city has been burned down a number of times, and even so recently as 1841. Nevertheless, the town that occupied the peninsula made by the river Nid and the Throndhjem fiord was an ancient borough when, in the year 997, King Trygvasen founded the city that is now known as Throndhjem, and I presume it is entitled to the honor of being considered venerable.

Throndhjem is one of the chief ports of Norway, and does a large business in the shipment of lumber and fish; but, except the cathedral, there is little to interest the traveler. This building, begun some time in the eleventh century, has been made upon no fixed plan, but has been added to and changed by a dozen hands. Some of the work, particularly the carving in stone, is very good, but many of its beauties have been hidden by the retaining walls that have been built up to support the original structure. The cathedral is now undergoing repairs, and in a few years will be in a more creditable condition than it now is, as the people of Norway are beginning to take a proper interest in its preservation. Beneath the altar of this church the body of St. Olaf was once buried, and the mortal part of Hardraada once rested here in the grave-yard; but no man can say where their bones are now.

We remained four days at Throndhjem, and had nearly determined upon a voyage to the North Cape, but the season had already grown late, and a cold rain-storm setting in, we concluded to defer the expedition to some more favorable time.

About three o'clock in the afternoon of July 28th, we entered the carriage to resume our journey, intending to make two stages before we should rest for the night. The first station was Esp, a splendid farm, with a very extensive outlook from the house over a well-cultivated country. A drive of a mile brought us down to the shore of the Throndhjem fiord, along which we passed until we reached Saltnusand, where we took rooms and ordered dinner. The latter part of the stage gives many beautiful views across the broad fiord, and the station is charmingly situated.

We were upon our way back across the Dovrefield, as it was our intention to reach Aak in the Romsdal, and we had selected a route through the valley of the Orkla, in order that we might avoid repeating more of the road than was necessary.

We were now in a part of the country where there was but little travel, and, as at each of the stations they were required to keep six horses, we did not find it necessary to make an early start to secure animals for the carriage. It was therefore at a reasonable hour the next morning that we proceeded upon our journey, but so heavy was the road and so steep the ascent to Ely, that we walked nearly the whole distance. Ely is situated on the summit of the range of hills that surrounds Throndhjem fiord, and the scene from this point is magnificent, the many sails in the harbor below adding life and interest to the picture.

The first half of the next stage was almost as bad as that we already had come over, but we shortly began the descent into the valley, and entered Orkladalsoren on a brisk trot, with a hot drag.

The station here promised something more than any we had yet seen, for the sign of " hotel " adorned the freshly-painted front. But the old traveler in Norway, who has been taught to place little confidence in signs, will not be surprised that we were unable to procure anything to eat, and were compelled to resort to our own stores.

While the horses were being put to the carriage, a number of rosy-cheeked children gathered round in wonder at the unusual magnificence of the equipage. I never saw finer children than those that are seen by the roadside in Norway; fat, cheery, blue-eyed cherubs. They grow up into handsome men and sturdy women.

I did not ask Johanssen what our bill was at the hotel for the use of the dining-room, but I am sure that it was a reasonable one, for the people of this country are not extortionate. We had a pair of very good horses up to By; one of them perhaps a little too fiery, but when the post-boy told me that he was past thirty, I entered no complaint in the "Day-book." This is a journal that is kept in accordance with law at each station, for the purpose of receiving any charges the traveler may make against the post-master or his servants. It is believed that formerly an officer inspected these books, and investigated the charges, but the entries of the modern tourists have proved so frivolous, they being nearly always complaints against the weather, that those made in the English language at least are now unheeded.

At Arlevald, a very neatly-kept farm-house, we stopped for the night. The next day we proceeded through Carlstadt to Grut. At this latter station we were shown the drinking-horn that has been used by many of the Norwegian monarchs as they passed from their coronation at Throndhjem, and as it was the custom for each to drop a piece of money into the cup, and as this coin was afterward used to ornament the horn, the owner has a valuable and interesting relic. I recollect that this drinking-horn was exhibited to us in the family room, and I thought that the bed, with its two rugs of sheepskin, that are used both winter and summer, did not look very inviting. Many of the richest farmers cling to the old custom of sleeping between robes of sheepskin or of fur, even though they may keep modern beds for their guests.

The next station was Haarstadt, and just beyond this is a beech-tree, celebrated over Norway for its size. I suppose that for a deciduous tree it is very large for the climate in which it grows, but I could not get up any very great amount of surprise at the sight of it.

The road, after we pass this station, leaves the valley, and by well-conducted turns climbs the steep mountain, many fine views being offered as we ascend. At the top of the hill we come again to Bjerkaker, and passing Austbjerg, we spend the night at Stuen, an excellent station.

The next day we make an early start, and by five o'clock in the afternoon have recrossed the Dovre-field, and have arrived at Dombass, in Gudbrands valley.

One stage up along the Laagen, and we reached Holaker, where we were to remain the next day, Sunday. The master of this station farms many acres, and owns large herds and flocks. The house is close by the road, about two hundred feet above the river, the corn-fields lying below it. The sæter-paths, upon which the cattle pass to and from the upland pastures, may be seen marking the steep mountain side.

This is one of the best stations in Norway from

which to make excursions after reindeer, as it is
but a short distance to the wildest parts of the
Dovre-field, and the sæter-huts will afford shelter
against the severe weather that is usual on those
heights. Most of the best salmon rivers in this
country are preserved, but in the proper season
the sportsman may shoot free, and quantities of
reindeer, black-cock, capercailzie, and other game
may be found on the mountains. The elk was
formerly an inhabitant of Norway, but, except on
the Swedish frontier, he is rarely to be seen.

While we were at Holaker a party of English-
men, with their guides, started out after reindeer.
One of the gentlemen, by stalking the animals,
which is, I believe, the usual custom, had killed
five during the previous season.

We were charmed with the hostess of our
inn, for she treated us as though we were welcome friends, and not strange wayfarers. The
amount of silver-plate that decorated our dinner
table seemed out of place in a farm-house. But
the Norwegian peasant is proud of his curiously
patterned silverware, and often has it in quanti-

ties that surprises the traveler. The silver gilt marriage-crown is everywhere sacredly kept, and handed down from generation to generation. Beautifully carved chests, hanging shelves, and smaller household articles of wood, made by the farmer during the long winter evenings, may be seen in even the poorest home. And many of the peasants are skillful workers in iron, while some will give to their steel knives the temper of a Damascus blade.

It was like parting with old friends when we bade adieu to these good people upon a bright Monday morning. A very pretty girl took the part of post-boy on this stage, all the males of the family being engaged in the hay-fields. The road to Holset led along that part of the river called the Lesje-vand, and at the next station, passing through the least interesting stage of our journey, we came to the lake, 2,000 feet above the sea, that is the common source of the Laagen, flowing south, and of the Rauma pouring down to the sea in another direction.

The next station is Molmen, and a short dis-

tance beyond it the road and the river begin that
fellowship that the narrowing valley compels
them to hold, until the gorge opens abruptly at
Aak. Before we reach Stuflaaten the Rauma
begins to descend very rapidly, forming beautiful
cataracts. After leaving this station we are well
into the Romsdal, celebrated throughout Norway
for its wild scenery. The road has been rapidly
falling, so that at Ormeim we are seven hundred
feet lower than at the last station.

Ormeim is in a narrow valley; lofty, almost
perpendicular, mountains rise upon either side of
the Rauma as it hurries down to the sea. From
the left a splendid torrent comes tumbling over
the top of the wall, and, spreading out into three
noisy falls, joins the rushing river.

Here we stay all night, in order that we may
have the bright morning sunshine to light up the
glories of the lower Romsdal.

When we look before us, after we leave Ormeim, the high mountains are so close together
that they seem to shut us in. At Fladmark we
reach the bottom of the valley.

But how shall I describe the Romsdal as it appeared to us at Horgheim? On either hand bare walls of black rock rise up to a height greater than six thousand feet. They threaten to close in upon us, and a sense of awe forces itself upon us as we look up at them. On the right the Horn rises symmetrically, while upon the left the Witches-peaks, sharp and clear, look like iron spikes on the almost level sky-line.

I can say no more. If in these few lines I do not convey an idea of the grandeur of the Romsdal, I am sure that I should do no better by multiplying words.

Three miles from the foot of the Horn the valley suddenly opens into a rough plateau, and here the Aak Hotel welcomes the traveler. Three miles beyond is the town of Veblungsnœs, upon the Romsdal fiord.

CHAPTER IV.

FROM AAK, THROUGH THE FIORDS, TO BERGEN.

THE solitary house at Aak, placed upon a slight eminence near the mouth of the gorge, has a beautiful and romantic situation. It is almost shut in by the high and bold mountains that have formed the gloomy valley through which we have just passed, while directly in front the tapering peak of the Romsdalhorn towers five thousand feet above the river. This hotel was originally the farm-house of Mr. Landmark, and has never been a station, but the great beauty of the situation has caused many travelers to take up their quarters here until their remunerative custom has induced the proprietor to make extensions to the modest homestead and improvements in the fare, until Aak has become one of the best inns in Nor-

way. There are many interesting excursions that
can best be made from this place, while the fishing
and hunting in the vicinity is not surpassed.
The royal salmon and reindeer's-flesh were the
standard dishes at Aak; the former taken daily
from the river that flows near the house, while
the venison, much inferior to that of the Vir-
ginia deer, was shot in the neighboring fields.

We found several charming ladies and some
jolly English collegians at Aak. Indeed, one may
expect to meet company here throughout the
season, not a disagreeable episode in a tour that
is, of a necessity, so quiet.

The short summer was drawing to a close, and
fearful lest we should be caught in the autumnal
rains before we got back to Christiania, we were
induced to leave this delightful place after a visit
of four days.

On one of the pleasant afternoons we drove to
Veblungsnœs, where we were, upon the next day,
to take the steamer to continue our tour. Veblungsnœs is a fishing village of eight or ten
houses that face upon its single street, few of
them the better looking for their evident age.

The inn, where we found shelter for the night was, however, both clean and comfortable.

During an evening walk upon the pier we saw how it is these dwellers on the shore become the hardy, brave sailors that they invariably are, for the children, many of them not above four or five years of age, had taken the fishing-boats and were rowing the crank shells about the deep waters of the fiord, and were thus early learning to despise the dangers of the waves. The steamer that lay at anchor, waiting for the morning to take us on our way, appeared hardly larger than the fishing-boats. The "Erkno," big enough perhaps for the requirements of the traffic she was engaged in, was, indeed, smaller than many pleasure yachts. She had been built to ply upon the Molde fiord and its branches, of which the Romsdal is the principal. Each of the main fiords has one or more of these vessels to take out to the sea-coast the products of the regions penetrated by these deep inlets, and larger ships, plying the length of the coast, carry their collected cargoes to the markets of Bergen or Throndhjem.

It was yet early, though the sun had been up some hours, when we were rowed out to the "Erkno," and shortly after we had reached the deck she was put in motion. We passed down the Romsdal fiord, hemmed in by the boldest shores we had yet seen, and which, even after we had seen the lower fiords, were remembered as very grand. From our starting point it is twenty-five miles to the junction with Molde fiord, and here the waters that have been scarcely a mile from shore to shore spread out until they form a bay ten miles in width.

Just before we reached Vœstnœs, where we were to disembark, we caught a distant view of the city of Molde, with its white houses standing out in strong relief against the green hills that rise beyond, the leper's hospital being dis- ' tinctly seen. Asylums for those unfortunate beings who are afflicted with leprosy have been established here and at Bergen. The disease does not exist in the interior of the country, but only affects the fishermen, and, it is supposed, is superinduced by the meager diet upon which they are forced to subsist.

A point of land hid Molde from our sight, and
an hour after noon we were landed at Vœstnœs.
Our carriage was soon ready for us, as it had not
been necessary to take it apart, and with a pair of
good horses we proceeded to cross over to the
Stor fiord.   The only object of interest in the first
stage of our journey was a ship-yard, where a
splendid vessel had just been launched.   It was
about seven miles of a heavy road that brought
us to the farm of Ellingsgard.   This being a
slow-station, where it is not compulsory for the
master to keep ready horses, we experienced some
delay.   At length two sorry beasts were released
from the plough and placed at our service.   We
passed slowly over the *field*, dotted with sœter-
huts, and after fourteen miles of a most uninteresting ride, we came to the smiling meadows that
lie about Soholt, and presently drew up before
that station lying upon the Stor fiord.

We found very good accommodations at Soholt, and after an early breakfast we took a row-
boat to meet the steamer that plies on the Stor
fiord, for there are no piers here, and the packet
will not wait long for the unexpected passengers,

The boats in which everything is carried between these steamers and the shore, at all the smaller ports, give the idea of being very insecure craft, but I have seen them carry well in heavy weather, owing largely, doubtless, to the seamanship of those who manned them.

The scenery about Soholt is not of a grand character, but as we steamed southwardly down the Stor fiord the mountains soon become imposing in height, rising abruptly from the water. After proceeding eight or nine miles we found the Dals fiord, trending eastward from the main artery. This fiord, resembling that part of the Stor fiord through which we had just passed, we followed to its head, some ten or twelve miles. It was here that Olaf, after one of his defeats, burned his last ship and fled through Valdalen. Upon the face of a cliff that rises from the water may be seen an irregular mark, that is said to have been left by a serpent thrown against the wall by this same holy Olaf. Turning about we again found the Stor, here called the Sunelvs fiord, and proceeded southwardly, the mountains becoming more precipitous as we advanced. On either side, at short intervals, we saw where the avalanches had scarred the rocks, sometimes having avoided the little farms that were cultivated upon the narrow ledges, sometimes having swept both farms and houses into the gulf beneath. Ten miles below the mouth of Dals fiord we reached the Geiranger fiord, which is considered the grandest in Norway. As we turned eastwardly to enter the narrow passage that presented itself, all that we had seen seemed insignificant with what we then beheld. The water is hardly more than a mile in width, while on either hand rise smooth rocks, with hardly a break in them, to a height of nearly five thousand feet, apparently even greater. The shadows blacken the surface of the fiord, and the waterfalls that plunge over the walls have a wierd whiteness. On the right a winding path, cut into the side of the cliff, leads to a house built upon a ledge where a venturesome mountaineer has sought to win a living from the little earth that has there found a resting place. We could well believe, as we were told by the master of our vessel, that the children were, for safety, tied to the door-posts, and that those of the family who died on the farm were lowered by ropes, a thousand feet, to the water below. Nine miles from its mouth, at the head of the fiord, is Maraak, where some of the passengers disembarked. The vessel was then put about, and in an hour we had again reached the Sunelvs fiord, and at its head, a half-hour's ride, we found the village of Helsylt, where we intended resting the next day.

It was nearly dark when we entered the inn at Helsylt, and we were too much fatigued with the journey of the past two days to make any observations of the place. Upon looking out of the window in the morning a beautiful sight met the eye. The fiord, lighted up by the morning sun, was alive with fairy-like sail-boats, that, at various distances, were making for the little beach made by the washings from the mountain side where the few houses that compose Helsylt find standing-room. As the foremost boats drew near we saw that they were filled with gaily-dressed peasants, and the tolling of the bell in the neighboring church reminded us that it was Sunday, and suggested the occasion of the ad-

vance of the flotilla. Upon leaving the inn we
found that mountains, almost as steep as those
that bordered the fiord, rose from behind the four
or five houses that were built upon the strand.
A road coming down through a deep valley
from the east passed by the door and climbed the
western hills; this and the fiord are the only
means by which Helsylt is accessible to the
outside world. Within an hour of our rising the
last boat had deposited its load upon the shore,
and in a body the people, now increased by oth-
ers who had come in by the road, quietly took
their way to church. It is only in such retired
spots as this that the peasants of Norway retain
the costume which was peculiar to different dis-
tricts, and was always, though rich in color, in
keeping with the dress of nature that surrounded
them. I am sure that a more lovely picture of
Norway and Norwegians could not have been
given us than that we had upon this glorious
summer day.

It had been our intention to proceed upon our
journey on Monday morning, but as I was de-
sirous of taking a good Norwegian pony home

with me, and having heard of a very fine speci-
men in Norangsdal, some thirty or forty miles
distant, I sent for the animal, and we awaited his
coming. Late in the evening of Monday my
messenger made his appearance with the pony.
" Per," for so he was called, pleased me so well
that I bought him at once, and though it was
through trouble and expense that I got him safely
to this country, I have never regretted my purchase. A friend found a mate for him at the
yearly fair in Holmen, and they make a most
serviceable and docile phæton team.

On Tuesday morning, then, we left Helsylt for
Faleidet, on the Nord-fiord, Mrs. Anderson and I
walking, while Johanssen and the post-boy (a
man nearly seven feet in height) helped the horses
drag the carriage up the cruelly steep hill. As
the first station, Tronstad, is twelve hundred feet
above our starting-point, we did not get much
assistance from the carriage, for it was load
enough in itself for the horses. When we got
a fresh pair, the road being better, we entered
the carriage and set forth. I led the pony from
my seat in the carriage, but as he was constantly

breaking away, I was glad to give him up at Haugen to a woman, who undertook to lead him, about fourteen miles, to Faleidet, for the sum of five Norsk dollars. I have not quite so good an opinion of this person as I have of Norwegians in general. She was the mistress of the station, and her house was so uninviting that we preferred eating our mid-day meal in the sunny pasture to going within her doors; and, in addition to this, I learned that instead of leading "Per," as she had covenanted, she mounted the poor beast, and trotted him the two stages that lie between Haugen and Faleidet.

Having got rid of our care, and the road proving a good one, we passed to Grodass at a brisk trot. This station is beautifully situated at the head of a lake called Horningsvand, and the road for some distance leads along the water side. But a hill soon interposed itself, and then for six or seven miles it was a dreary, upward, uninteresting stage. Finally we reached the crest of the mountain and began the descent, the last mile into Faleidet being as near the perpendicular as will allow the stones to lie upon the surface. At last, wet and weary, after a most fatiguing journey of about thirty-five miles, we reached the station, which proved an excellent one.

It was with a sense of relief that we woke to the fact that we were to complete our journey to Bergen by boat, and that we should not again have to trust ourselves to the rough by-roads that connect the fiords. All that I have said heretofore in regard to the admirable state in which the roads of Norway are kept, refers to the highways between important points and where fast stations are kept. But in passing through the thinly populated country between Vestnœs and Faleide there is much vexation of spirit and of body

It was about nine o'clock in the morning when we went aboard the "Sogne" steamer, to pass through the Nord-fiord and down the coast to Bergen. The storm that had caught us the preceding day had not yet passed off, but under the canopy stretched over the quarter-deck we were comparatively comfortable. Among the passengers we were pleased to see people with whom we had occasionally met in different parts of the country, among them two English ladies who were traveling, unaccompanied by male escort, without inconvenience or annoyance. After casting off the cables we steamed across the fiord to Udvik, a charmingly situated village skirting a little bay, and surrounded by fine mountains. After leaving Udvik a few miles, we caught a glorious view of the Justedal glacier, the emerald-green ice rising even with the high peaks, and throwing out light from its glittering face. This glacier, it is asserted, is seventy miles in extent; and in some places the ice is several thousand feet in thickness.

I do not know whether I can speak of the Nord-fiord as I should, and yet be true to my love for the Geiranger. Certainly many of the views upon the Nord are indescribably grand, and yet entirely different from that of any other inlet we had yet visited. The majestic mountains rise gradually from the water, and the lower parts are covered with farms and forests, while the tops rise in gloomy sterility. Indeed, each of the fiords we visited had scenery peculiar to itself, and always, on this western coast, magnificent. Night closed in upon us before

we had left the fiord, and when we came upon
the deck in the morning we were sailing through
the canals that are formed along the coast by
the innumerable islets that extend throughout
its length, and so break the force of the angriest
seas. These islands are for the most part bare
rocks, but here and there may be seen one that
affords some grass to a few stunted cows. About
four o'clock in the afternoon we overtook a fleet
of fishing-boats, built like the old serpent ships
of the Norsemen, carrying their cargoes to Bergen, and shortly afterward—a welcome sight—
we saw the red-tiled roofs of the city spread over
the little plat of ground that is shut off from the
interior by steep, brown hills, and almost shut
out from the ocean by the islands that lie across
the mouth of the bay.

CHAPTER V.

IT is not often that the traveler will have three
successive days at Bergen without rain, for the
climate of this place is exceedingly moist. We
were, however, fortunate in having pleasant
weather during our stay. Bergen has a queer,
cramped, old-fashioned look that makes it an interesting city to the traveler from the New World.
The principal street is the Strand, which, though
lined with very well filled shops, is only wide
enough for two carts to pass each other, and I do
not know how vehicles change their direction

58

except by going around a block, or by meeting with one of the open squares, of which there are several. The narrow streets running parallel with each other are connected by the narrowest of alleys, called " smugs," a name that suggests their appearance. The city has about thirty thousand inhabitants, and is built upon both sides of a little harbor called the Vaagen, the older part occupying the left hand shore as one approaches, and here are Hakon's Hall and Walkendorff's tower, relics of the thirteenth century. In this part of the city, facing the harbor, may be seen the tall, white warehouses built and once occupied by the merchants of the Hanseatic League, now store-houses for the fish that are brought from Nordland. The city is by no means well built, the houses being of wood, and few of them more than two stories in height; the architecture is of the most primitive character.

Bergen was once the richest and most important city of the three Northern Kingdoms, and the excellence of its harbor, and the great and increasing fish trade of Norway, will no doubt restore this port to its former prosperity. The value of the fish product sent from Bergen to the various foreign countries amounts to about ten millions of dollars annually, nearly one-third of the sum received into the country from its combined exports. The views from the neighboring hills, the museum, the fish-market, and the fur stores are the objects of interest in Bergen. The collection of specimens of sea-life in the museum is one of the most extensive and best prepared of any in Europe, while the furs to be found in this city are much finer than those I saw in London.

A storm had just set in when, early upon the 15th day of August, we went aboard the " Hardangeren " steamer, to continue our projected tour ; and I am satisfied, from what I have learned of that climate, that after the phenomenon of three dry days the same deluge continues to flood the streets of Bergen.

The city was soon buried in a thick fog as we steamed out among the rocky islands gathered about the mouth of the harbor. Our course then lay south, through channels such as had offered us approach to Bergen from the north, the water being perfectly still, though the North Sea, with such a wind as swept by us, must have been raving on the outside of the barrier.

It was already afternoon when we entered the Hardanger fiord, and the lofty mountain-tops were hidden in the clouds. About four o'clock the mist lifted, and while daylight lasted we did not lose any of the grand panorama that was unrolled before our eyes. The chief beauty of the Hardanger fiord lies in the richness and variety of its foliage, which, until its eastern arms are reached, covers the very summits, here and there a bare point being the exception. It was between some of these higher peaks that we caught a glimpse of the " Folge-fond," a glacier nearly as extensive as the Justedal.

It was late in the night when we reached Eide, at the head of the fiord, and as there was no promise of a fair morrow, we left the steamer, which was the next day to proceed down the Stor-fiord, and so abandoned our plan of exploring that inlet and a half-formed design of attempting a visit to the Voring-fos, one of the finest water-falls in Europe.

But the wisdom of our decision was apparent

in the morning, when we saw the fog lying thick and low, obscuring the view, and the rain pouring down in torrents that took away all desire to see the Voring-fos. The rainy season had set in, and we had much to look at and far to go before we reached Christiania. After an early breakfast we took the carriage, expecting to reach Gudvangen, on the Nero fiord, before nightfall. For some distance we drove along the shores of a little lake that tempted us to stay and admire it. But we had a long day's ride before us, and we resisted all attempts to detain us. At an ill-kept station, called Vasenden, we got a pair of fresh horses, and a short distance beyond we began to ascend the "Skiervet." There are some splendid views from this point, and half-way up the hill the road is carried across the stream in the face of a beautiful water-fall. After passing "Skiervet" we came to a pine forest, then to farms and meadows until fourteen miles from Eide, we drew up before Fleischer's hotel in Vossvangen.

This little village has, from the distance, a very picturesque appearance, the ancient stone church being the principal feature in the landscape.

The inn at Vossvangen is a very good one, and as the neighborhood furnishes excellent sport for both rod and gun, it is a favorite resort of the English tourist, who is always ready to cast a fly or " blaze away " at a ptarmigan.

We remained only a few hours at Vossvangen, notwithstanding its varied attractions, and then set forward. The rain was still pouring down, and as the road for the next stage was a very heavy one, we were compelled to walk almost the whole distance to Tvinde, seven miles, and a great part of the way to Vinje, the next station beyond. Here no fresh horses were to be found, and we waited until the pair that had just arrived from a journey of fifteen miles, over one of the worst roads in Norway, should be rested sufficiently to repeat the exertion. This delay would not have been disagreeable under more favorable circumstances, but the only house at the station was so greatly in need of sweeping, that we preferred remaining in the carriage until the post-boy should agree to go forward, to seeking the shelter that was offered us.

At length the horses were put to the carriage

and we toiled on to Stalheim, which is twelve
hundred feet above Eide. A short distance beyond this station the road descends into the Nero-
dal, a wonderful piece of engineering, for it is
carried nearly a thousand feet in the distance of
half a mile by fourteen bends, that are built up
in solid masonry against the mountain's face.
On each side of this work is a fine water-fall, first
the one and then the other being presented as the
traveler follows the turns of the terraces. At
the foot of Stalheim-cliff the valley is only wide
enough for the road to find a bed alongside of the
little stream, the mountains on both hands rising
perpendicularly. Night caught us in this pass,
gloomy enough in the brightest day, but the
horses knew their way, and we pushed on to
Gudvangen, although everything was enveloped
in darkness.

It is through this gorge that the New fiord
comes up to Gudvangen, and the narrowness and
winding of its channel gives it in many places the
appearance of a lake set deep in the mountains.
It is often difficult for the traveler to predict where
the outlet lies, and what the course will be, for

sometimes the steepest mountain that blocks the way will seem to move aside and open a passage. It was down this magnificent scenery that we passed, the morning after we had reached Gudvangen, in the steamer that plies the Sogne-fiord and its branches. Innumerable water-falls surrounded us, many of them leaping without a break from the *fields* into the fiord below, and adding to the mystic grandeur of the scene. After passing a few miles we met the Aurland fiord, the channel becoming much wider, but the mountains still very grand. Fifteen miles from Gudvangen we gain the Sogne-fiord; this, the largest fiord in Norway, stretches more than a hundred miles into the land. The scenery along its whole length is said to be majestic, and more of the interior of the country is presented from it than from the confined inlets I have been describing. We traversed fifteen miles of this fiord to Lerdalsoren, between mountains that were striking in form and of great altitude. The highest part of the *field* in Sogne-fiord is the peak of " Bleien," which rises about eight thousand feet above the water.

We disembarked at Lerdalsoren, and once more taking the carriage we were driven up to the inn, about a mile from the pier.

As the weather continued bad, and prevented our making any of the excursions from this place, we left it the morning after our arrival by the road leading up the Lerdal, over the Fille-field, and finally through the beautiful Valders.

It was but a very short distance that the way led over the level plain; before we had passed over the first stage we had already entered a valley, which, before we came to Husum, had become a wild gorge, with masses of rock broken into weird shapes, hanging over the way and forbidding our approach. The river sometimes rushes along by the roadside, then having leaped into a chasm, is heard chafing against its walls far below us.

About half way between the second and third stations we passed the old church of Borgund. This edifice, said to be eight hundred years old, is fantastically built of wood, now black with age, and, with its broken roof and gables adorned with dragon's heads, suggests China rather than Norway. Beyond this the valley widens again, and at Hœg we reach the foot of the Fille-field, though the Lerdal river, now fifteen hundred feet above the sea, still keeps us company. The road thus far has, though admirably built, been alternately climbing and descending, but before we arrived at Maristuen, we were forced to gain nearly two thousand feet in the four or five miles.

Maristuen, besides being a station, is one of the houses built by government for the safety and comfort of those travelers who may be crossing the *field* in bad weather, and the keeper has certain privileges from the state for living in this bleak and lonely spot. Nystuen, the next station, also supported by the government, is the highest point in the pass. That part of the *Fille-field* over which we have come is a dreary waste, but has not the wildness and variety that characterized the *Dovre-field*. Several fine peaks rise about Nystuen, from one of which the range of the Jotunfield, the loftiest mountains in Norway, may be seen.

The people who pass the long and severe winters upon these exposed heights must suffer great hardships, and lead a life of tiresome monotony. For many days they dare not, in the deep snows and biting winds, leave the shelter of the house, and the only strangers they are likely to meet are those who probably require their ready aid. The keeper of this station has been rewarded by the state with a medal for his humane exertions in saving the lives of many poor wayfarers who have been caught in the dreaded snow-storms, and it must be a wild night that would imprison him should he believe that there were travelers upon the road. It was but a few days after the middle of August, and we were warmly clothed, yet I shiver now as I recollect how cold it was the night we passed at Nystuen.

I have elsewhere spoken of the difficulty in procuring good food while traveling in this country, a trouble that lies more in the carelessness of the people than in any want of material. Most of the station-keepers are rich farmers, who own their herds of cattle and flocks of sheep, but as they do not care for greater variety of food than they have been accustomed to, they think it unreasonable in the traveler to ask for more. Although there were a number of fowls about the farm at Nystuen, no one knew where the eggs were, and it created surprise when a demand was made for one of the chickens to be served at breakfast.

The descent of the Fille-field had very much the same scenery as we saw upon the farther side, but the speed with which we hurried down the long hills was much more pleasant than the slow progress we had been making. Skogstad, at the eastern foot of the Fille-field, introduces us into the district known as Valders, an uninterrupted series of lovely vales, extending more than seventy-five miles.

From Skogstad the road leads down to a lake, and then bordering it for seven miles, brings us to Tune. A short distance from this latter station is a view which an " American gentleman," so said the delighted station-master, has pronounced to be the finest in the world. I do not think that I can conscientiously say that I coincide in the opinion, but I think that he is not far wrong. From Tune to Oilo the old road led over the Kvamskleven, and still stands as a monument to the skill and labor of those who have recently cut a level road in the face of the solid granite along the side of the lake. The views from this station are very extensive, and to those who have just left the grand but bare and dark fiords, these smiling vales are very charming.

From Oilo the road crosses the stream to Stee, and then, passing along another lake, brings us to Reien. The scenery for the whole of the day's journey to Lillestrand, where we stopped for the night, is beautiful beyond the power of description; so broad, so varied, with wooded glens, rolling pastures, silver lakes, and awe-inspiring mountains.

At Reien we saw, as we had often before seen like cases, the disadvantage of traveling in this country without an interpreter. We found, upon arriving at the station, two German gentlemen who had long been detained because, there being no horses, they could not express a willingness to pay for horses taken from the farm. After Johanssen had caused our wants to be supplied, he put the strangers in the way of getting on in the world.

Lillestrand is a very good station, but we did not long enjoy its comforts, for upon learning that there were so many travelers on the road that we should make an early start if we did not wish to risk delay, Johanssen, who appeared to be sleepless as well as tireless, called us at three o'clock, and in an hour afterward we were upon the road. The drive to Fagernœs, leading around the Strand-fiord, had scenery equal to that which we had enjoyed the day previous, and I am almost tempted to pronounce the same verdict upon the view from the hill beyond Frydenlund that the " American gentleman " rendered for the one near Oilo. After passing Gravdal the road began to descend, and we drove the ten miles from Tomlevolden to Odnœs, down the valley of the Etna, in an hour.

Upon the following morning we took the steamer at Odnœs, and passing through the Rands fiord, a lake fifty miles in length, bordered with fields of grain, we were landed at the terminus of the railroad, on its southern end. Here, taking the waiting train, we were hurried past the falls of Honefos, along the base of Ringriget, through Drammen, and at ten o'clock that night were installed in luxurious apartments at the Victoria Hotel, Christiania.

CONCLUSION.

NORWAY is, according to the constitution, "a free state, independent, indivisable, and inalienable, united to Sweden under the same king." Previous to 1814 it had been under the domination of the kings of Denmark for nearly five centuries, but in that year Prince Christian, of Denmark, was elected king, to abdicate within six months in favor of Charles XIII, of Sweden, who had been foreed upon the country by the decision of the "allied powers," and who was then finally accepted by representatives of the people. This king was succeeded by his heir, Beenadotte, under the title of Charles John

XIV, and it is the grandson of Napoleon's mar-
shal, the wisest and ablest monarch in Europe,
who is now at the head of the government.
There are no longer any titles of nobility, and the
people are boastful of their liberty, but they have
the sincerest love and loyalty for their sovereign,
whose portrait may be seen in nearly every cot-
tage.

The parliament is elected, for three years, from
among the people, and the upper house is chosen
by the Stor-thing from its own body. It has
about the same powers as our congress, and a bill
that passes three successive Stor-things become
the law even against the veto of the king.

The Norwegians are an intelligent, sober, and
honest race, who prosper in a country that is little better than a range of rocky mountains; the
forests and fisheries only making it possible for
two millions of people to find support. No more
than twelve hundred square miles is devoted to
the cultivation of grain; about five times that
area is in valley and upland pasture.

From the nature of the country, affording so
many inaccessible retreats for wild beasts, Nor-

way will long continue to furnish sport for the hunter, while every small stream is stocked with trouts, and the larger ones are filled with salmon. Bears, elk, and reindeer may still be found in sufficient numbers to reward their chase, while birds identical with the Scotch game are everywhere plentiful. The right of fishery belongs to the proprietors of the banks, but there is no difficulty in the stranger obtaining permission to cast a fly. Except during the " close season " the sportsman may wander over the *fields* at his own will.

The most pleasant season for traveling in Norway is from the middle of June to the middle of August, and there is much of the finest scenery that can be visited in a tour of a few days from either Christiania or Bergen. Stockholm is only distant thirty-six hours by rail from the former of these cities.

I have avoided permitting myself to be led into any reference to the traditions of Norway, for had I been tempted to follow my predilections, the little book that I now offer would have grown into many large volumes. The " Varanger " of Stamboul, the Vikings of coastal Europe, and the

Normen of France were heroes who furnished unfailing subjects for song and story. I will, I hope, be pardoned if I now depart from my resolution, and append a version of the circumstances of the death of the most remarkable personage that appears in the history of Norway; a soldier of fortune, who was beloved by a queen of the East, who was a king by purchase, and who lost his life in an attempt to become possessed of the English crown:

THE BATTLE OF STAMFORD-BRIDGE.

'Tis "Ho! For England. For rich and ruddy England.
  Ho! For England." With cries the harbor rings.
    Hardrada's fleet is sailing,
    Foredooming woe and wailing,
And eager for the slaughter the Raven spreads her wings.

With thrice ten thousand Norsemen, they fill a thousand
        war-ships,
  To follow Harold's banner, " The Waster of the Land."
    The river-mouth is carried,
    Northumbria is harried;
And then before the walls of York they scatter Morcar's
        band.

Five hundred men in hostage will meet the King at
    Stamford.
  At Stamford-bridge Hardrada waits; his men have
      blade and spear;
      They deem no harm can find them,
      Their byrnies left behind them;
Defenseless then they bow to fate without a warning
    fear.

But see, from out the westward, that cloud of dust arising;
    " Here comes no friends, but armed foes," the wily
      Tostig cries;
    " There Saxon Harold's riding;
    This is no place for biding,
We'll seek our byrnies and our ships, in haste, if we be
    wise."

" We passed the stormy ocean to find this day and meet-
    ing,
    And here we wait to see the end, whatever may be-
      tide.
    We'll make them keep their distance,
    While from our ships assistance
Shall straight be called—on fleetest steeds our messen-
    gers shall ride."

So spake the Northern Harold, and then arrayed his
    spearmen,
  Shield lapping shield, from right to left, they form
    an iron ring.
  Within are placed the bowmen,
  Who first assail the foemen
As on they come, with gleaming front, led by the En-
    glish King.

Like lightning come the Saxons, like thunder is their
    charging,
  Their horses' breasts are braced against the well-sup-
    ported shields.
  No break betrays the Norsemen
  As quick they spear the horsemen,
Who fall before them like the grain when thrall the
    sickle wields.

Back ride the sullen Saxons, with broken ranks retreat-
    ing.
  Ah! well for Harold had his men their ardor kept in
    bounds;
  But when they see them turning,
  With eager courage burning,
They break the ring and charge the foe like fierce and
    famished hounds.

And in the front of battle they keep no form or order:
  Each seeks a foeman for his sword, to kill where'er he
      can.
    Ah! fatal was that sally,
    They strive in vain to rally,
As on them falls the Saxon horse and slays them man by
      man.

There strides the fated Harold, his path is strewn with
      corses;
  He cleaves his way through mailed ranks, deals many
      a deadly blow.
    Oh, Emma, wert thou holding
    Him in thy metal folding,
That arrow ne'er had pierced his neck that laid Hardrada
      low.

And yet the Raven banner is waving in defiance,
  Where gather Norway's boldest who fight to save the
      day.
    Then would they turn a flying
    When Tostig lay a dying,
But from the ships the Gorcock comes to join the dread-
      ful fray.

Too late, oh gallant Eystein, you stem the tide of battle.
  On, on the conquering Saxons sweep against the weary
      host.

Naught now is left but glory,
Thy bout shall live in story;
A hundred spears let out thy life, and Norway's field is
   lost.

Turn from the scene of slaughter, where feed the wolf
   and vulture,
   Where Harold lies unclaimed, unknown, amid his
   heaps of slain,
   There England in thy keeping
   Is cause for Norway's weeping,
Her bravest sons unburied lie upon thy bloody plain.

With thrice ten thousand Norsemen they filled a thou-
   sand war-ships,
   To follow Harold's banner, " The Waster of the Land."
   Back now the fleet is sailing,
   And soon there will be wailing,
But four and twenty ships return with Harold's broken
   band.

www.ingramcontent.com/pod-product-compliance
Lightning Source LLC
Chambersburg PA
CBHW020332090426
42735CB00009B/1500